Treading Shallow Waters

MELLENE HEDERIAN

photographs also by
Mellene Hederian

For my mother, Roberta.

CONTENTS: 46 poems

Part I

ACKNOWLEDGMENTS

➤ I'd like to first thank, albeit posthumously, my parents Roberta and John for praising my writing all my life and for always letting me know they were proud of me. What I wouldn't give to hear those words from their lips today. May they rest in peace.

➤ Thank you to my husband Jimmy Reilly for his endless patience, generous heart, acoustic serenades, and well-timed levity.

➤ To my brother Darin, thank you for your strength, your love, and your friendship. When we were little, I always wanted to carry you everywhere, and all this time, it's been you carrying me. To his wife Serena, you are truly the sister I never had! I love you and your beautiful children Robbie and Reese so much it hurts.

➤ To my aunt Connie Lufrano, thank you for dropping everything to mother me when I've needed mothering.

➤ To the friends of a lifetime, Dorianne Bible and Jen McKeon, thank you for the closeness of family, the endless support, and oh, so much wine!

➤ To all my friends and colleagues at Jericho High School, including but not limited to:

Elissa Cosenza, Trish Gulitti, Michael Kramer, Denise Ryder, and Charu Vardhan, thank you for always being there for me personally and professionally, and for generously supporting this project. Trish and Denise, I'll always remember your help and encouragement.

➢ Special thanks to Dr. Michael Hartnett for his insightful feedback and editing, and his predilection for the long dash. Thank you to the lovely and talented Danielle Randone for her rendition of Vincent van Gogh's *The Starry Night*.

➢ Heartfelt thanks and deep admiration to author Chris Benedict, who is the main reason this project of mine ever came to fruition. Without your courage first, I might not have found my own. I am forever grateful for your fortitude, assistance, and friendship.

➢ Thank you Jericho alumni Justin Einhorn, Nolan Aibel, and Oren Weismann, three students who, simply by being their remarkable selves, have renewed my love of teaching, writing, and living.

➢ I'm forever thankful that poetry is a form of teaching and teaching is a form of poetry. And finally, I am thankful for the serendipity of the universe, which I don't believe is random, for all things – large or small – happen for a reason.

Treading Shallow Waters

Why I read poetry

The most inconceivable,

intolerable pain

I've ever endured

was not physical.

It did not pierce my skin,

nor tear the flesh,

nor burn the surface,

but spread

instead

an insidious pestilence throughout me,

awakening my senses

to senseless, unjust suffering.

The cruelest,

most inhumane acts

I've ever witnessed

were not inflicted by an enemy.

The perpetrator was poetry.

She held me captive against my will

opening my own wounds

and adding to their tenderness

the horrors

dead strangers have felt.

Tens of thousands of others—

my nameless brothers and sisters,

whose agony,

heartbreak,

loss,

regret,

remorse,

and despair

are immortalized

into perfect words

on a page.

Poem after poem,

I ingest the pulsating poison.

She courses through me

and

    I lose my lover to a landmine,

and

    I am maimed in battle

    fighting a war I don't understand,

and

    I bury my child who has died of cancer,

and

    endure the familiar pangs of

    unrequited love.

Poem after poem

she seduces with sardonic sensations

and

    I find out I am barren,

and

    I rue the day I entered this marriage,

and

    I bid farewell to my most precious dreams,

and

    I embrace the abuse

    because it's all I know of love,

and

    I cut myself to prove I'm still alive,

and

    I visit my parents' graves.

Stockholm syndrome:

both euphoric and trapped,

I owe all the joy I know to the pain.

Two worlds

I walked alone at the beach today.

The sand—

too hot;

the air—

too humid.

I tried to look for you,

but the sun's stare was unforgiving.

I whispered your name once, then shouted it.

Did you hear me

over the thoughtless crash

of waves?

Hurt

My

very

life

causes me to ache.

Waves of sorrow

sweep and surge about

tossing me carelessly

into musky,

squalid caverns

I dare not pass through.

There is only dust, despair, and darkness.

My very life:

a torrent of raw,

paralyzing numbness,

sends me grudgingly soaring

over glorious snow-tipped mountaintops,

adorned with the furtive kisses

of an army of unforeseen lemon-yellow daisies,

a home

to a thousand proud eagles,

only to abandon me there,

far from myself and alone.

I am amputated,

dissected,

fitful,

bruised,

writhing.

The blunt force

of each

inconsiderate day

touches the tenderest spots—

bastardizing

and butchering

my countless tomorrows.

Antisocial media

I worry about humanity's sanity

when actors on a television show called 'Glee'

O.D.

When we perpetuate ignorance and hate

on Facebook and Twitter;

we're making things worse

instead of making them better.

When children are cyberbullied

so badly

they end their lives madly

with belts in their bedrooms,

leaving in their wake a cloudy mushroom.

Crest-fallen, disappointed,

when the zombies reach our doors

we blame those we have appointed.

Every day is a chance to start

healing our wounds,

but we only do that which will beckon our doom.

Quick to prove ourselves right

but not

to say we're sorry.

There's a headline every day

redirecting my worry.

We teach history, not the present,

for it's too controversial.

We ignore our own faults

like they're just the commercials.

If we don't start looking,

will we ever find it?

If we don't call something wrong,

will we ever mind it?

Fiancés and sons

Have you ever shared a favorite song

with your fiancé or son?

Only to receive a lackluster response,

say –

or none?

Those students in your classes

who read

poems

too rapidly

sound like robots

running low

on

their

Duracell

batteries.

They are the same children computing

on the cloud

who cannot unshroud the shuffled

songs in their palms.

I know they are listening,

but what do they hear?

Sure, they have earbuds in their ears.

There was that one day his dad asked

him to come downstairs.

The older man put the Beatles on,

the younger, stood there—

awkward in his adolescence,

blind to it:

listening, not hearing.

Like how some cords run just short of

the wall,

the ear does not reach the soul for all.

Half-hearted

Invited to society's birthday party,

I went.

Didn't want to feel guilty about not going;

can't say I looked forward to it.

Nursed my drink,

which nursed my sorrow,

which nursed my insecurities.

Kissed friends hello, enemies, too,

and wondered, indifferent,

if they could tell the difference.

Half-hearted happiness abounds:

when even at society's birthday party

misery thrives and nobody sees.

Half-hearted happiness abounds:

when

even at society's birthday party we

use the word "love" more often about

the cake,

the clothes,

the hair,

than about people.

Half-hearted happiness abounds:

when

even at society's birthday party we

can't put down our cell phones,

our troubles, our masks, our mistakes,

and just live in the moment.

I received the invitation, society,

I guess I'll be there.

I "love" cake.

Roots

Kinsmen and brethren all resembling me,

roots begin our breath unseen and unknown.

Kindling branching off every family tree

though our forest desolate, undergrown.

A couple of saplings exchange an oath,

and summer's grassy splendor casts its spell.

And new seedlings spring creating new growth,

because of these joys no one heard the knell.

Some branches can't be nurtured and repaired!

How envious the poor starling must be!

For this, there is no way to be prepared.

You pulled the roots right out from under me.

–What you took, I cannot have another.

Too soon pulled: my father and my mother.

Long distance

I sat down at her kitchen table—

strewn with Amazon boxes

and unopened mail

and unused gift cards.

Her twenty-something son was home.

I broke the cards. She lit a candle.

I wondered if mediums could read truths

on a face

or gather facts from a phone call.

She doesn't know my last name.

And then her gift came to her.

What probably tormented her as a child but has

served her ever since:

I see a man on your father's side...

But he's not your father.

Yes. A grandfather I never knew.

And a woman?

But not your mother.

Right again, I said.

I see another woman, but she's not your mother.

Yes, I said. My aunt.

Feeling both cold and hot, I thought:

What am I doing here?

And then this magical operator,

witch of two worlds made me a believer.

In ghosts

and in gifts.

Oh. You're mother's here.

She's pushed them all aside.

She wants to talk.

The errand

Your sympathy card arrived today:

the one a stranger was paid to write

and who didn't know my mother.

As I read it I wondered:

Did you drive to the store to buy

only that card?

Fight back tears selecting it?

Have trouble filling it out?

Or did you pick up a toothbrush, too?

Woe is I

Heartbreak can be gradual or at once.

I know because I've greeted woeful days.

The healing can take weeks; often months:

We, walking dead, subsist in impotent haze.

Cracks in a windshield, like a spider's web:

Reflected in the mirror is not me.

Pretending it's a natural flow and ebb,

I trudge through moments of monotony.

A steady numbness starts its long reside,

Compelling silent screams for a release.

Like Romeo, Act I, I want to hide.

I wonder when my languishing will cease.

I long for finer days when we are free,

when life provides more time for you and me.

Let down

Like a foul stench,

disappointment lingers

making me sob

and sigh

and suffocate on disappointment.

Wanting what is not yours and wondering why.

Not wanting what your reality is

but having no choice.

Being let down.

A spoiled surprise.

More toxic than being told lies.

The incorrigible "no" when you paid for a "yes."

What matters to you doesn't matter to them.

Being told "I just can't"

when you know they certainly could.

Case closed before you've told the jury—

    what jury?

One was never assembled.

Such a let-down

that we are so utterly careless.

Don't we know

nothing hurts worse than unfairness?

Shortchanged: left feeling dazed and listless—

Disrespect is akin to injustice.

Alzheimer's

Your poison spread slowly,

first making cloudy his memory

of what he had for lunch today.

"A common occurrence," the coward in you says.

Ashamed, yet amused,

he'd shake his head and laugh out loud:

"Holy shit—I honestly can't remember."

Months zip by and dozens of lunches

are forgotten.

Tuna fish sandwiches

with pickles and cold slaw,

gone forever, like photos in a fire

collapsing to ash.

We'd catch him shaving his face in the bathroom.

Confused,

instead of shaving cream he's using deodorant

rubbing the solid, Old Spice stick on his cheeks.

He lost his cell phone

and got lost in his car,

driving aimlessly on highways during the night.

Losing both privileges,

he devolved into a punished teenager.

Next you invaded his vocabulary.

At first stealing words like

incidental,

envious,

occasionally.

Frustrated,

he would search for alternatives

and manage to be understood.

But your appetite grew stronger

and your poison spread further

evaporating from his tongue

thirsty,

help,

pencil.

Stumbling, angry, embarrassed, and afraid,

My father would scratch and claw

to express himself:

a persistent mouse on a wheel

spinning toward escape he can taste.

Without the pride of a grown man

who ran a business,

raised a family,

owned a home,

found the family dog 10 blocks away.

Without a clue

of how long

this hell on earth would last.

"Senior moments," "CRS," and "getting old"

are the Bazooka Joe labels we stick on you,

when

donning

skull and crossbones

would be more truthful.

Like a gutless thief in the night,

you plundered

an old man's memory and thoughts,

taking

what little joy in living he had left.

You robbed him

of every life treasure.

Nostalgia.

Reminiscence.

Conversation.

Autonomy.

Friendships.

Satisfaction.

Closure.

Pride.

Independence.

Dignity.

And eventually,

my name.

Funeral dress

Thank you.

I see that you picked up my dress

from the cleaners—

The navy blue dress with fine, white dots

that fits like a glove

and just passes the knee.

I once loved that dress—

and chose it on purpose.

Its pattern

matches the tie my dad wears eternally.

The deep navy blue like the endless night sky;

the dots: icy hot stars.

Fishing online

The friendly man's voice on the phone,

warm with living and loving,

learned to be careful when fishing online.

Harvey was his name, and I'd never heard of him.

He said he'd been trying

to track down my father—

a college friend of his—

to invite him to a special event.

He didn't know his number

or his current address,

but he'd remembered his contagious laugh

and his good heart.

After some fishing online he'd found me,

His daughter.

And her blog.

And a eulogy.

Old men should be careful when fishing online

for their long-lost college friends.

His friend John,

78,

the one with the contagious laugh

and the good heart,

will not be able to attend.

But only a little

Ending you and me is hard.

Like pushing away my plate before I'm full.

Like reading the last page of a good book.

Like that hazy sort of sadness

when guests leave a party too early.

Missing you and me hurts.

I feel it in every atom, every pore.

I'm the stump that remains

after the tree has been felled;

the saddest baggage on the belt—

unclaimed.

Remembering me and you is a drug

that replaces the here and now

with the there and then.

Like watching my favorite movie,

pausing at the good parts: rewind, play, repeat.

Just imagining your face helps.

Just recalling what you think of me helps.

Defining what "me and you" means helps.

But only a little.

Sick Days

I'm not sick anywhere a doctor can heal me.

My head doesn't throb.

I don't have a fever.

My stomach feels fine.

It's not something I ate.

I'm getting plenty of sleep, in fact,

it's all I do;

it's all I want to do.

I just want my bed.

Today–

and tomorrow.

I'm not sick.

The way my days drag

their

bloated,

sagg-

ing

selves

through the week,

carrying their feeble

numbers on their backs.

We're all very impressed.

You eat,
you drink,
you piss,
you wash,
you dress,
you do,
you work,
you sit,
you drive,
you walk,
you read,
you breathe,
you eat,
you drink,
you watch,
you talk,
you drive,
you drink,
you sigh,

you sleep,
you sleep,
you sleep.

I'm not sick, but

the hours in my days don't seem real,

the way they ooze,

drip,

and con-

geal.

Stop asking me how I feel.

I'm not sick.

Crying in

The poison only circulates,

traveling the avenues of pain and possibility.

The mask I wear fits poorly

and identifies as a mask.

This locomotive is unforgiving;

the stops:

never my choosing.

We-lurch-ahead-at-such-a-speed-that-my-view-
out-my-window-is-one-long-psychedelic-
nauseating-paint-smear.

The conductor is wicked

and doles out more.

His turns are right angles.

I dare not pull the handle.

I dare not look.

I swallow hard.

Like a rubber band expected to hold

one

too

many

books in a bundle,

I feel the urge to snap—

from the many months of this wild ride

crying in.

Crying out

Everyone knows what ugly crying feels like:

fire in your throat,

sandpaper in your swollen, bloodshot eyes.

Everyone knows what ugly crying feels like:

head throbbing

and heart splintering

from the panic

and the pain

and the pressure.

Everyone knows what ugly crying feels like:

intense and wrong.

Shut-the-door-and-no-one-come-in ugly.

A too familiar, unpleasant experience.

The precursor?

Loss devastating, rejection cold, injustice blatant.

The aftermath: exhaustion.

The sweet release of salt and bitterness,

leaving in its wake

mascara on a pillowcase

and peace.

Grief

I could easily

slip into the grief

just like a warm bath,

treading those shallow waters

and never coming clean.

I could easily

close the door

and let the hot water run,

so that when I enter

and my raw skin touches the surface,

it scalds at first

as it opens my pores

and the hurting seeps in.

I could easily

turn back the clock to when I was a child.

Shrinky-dink my way

back to ten o'clock curfews

and telephone cords,

sitcoms

and Sunday dinners.

I could be like those sad people you see on TV

who self-medicate their loss with gain,

trying to bandage their gaping wounds

with garage sale bargains and

vintage board games.

I could easily

spend all my days allowing my loss

to envelop my life;

become my landlord.

But I choose not to.

It's why I take showers.

Cold ones.

Part II

Why I write poetry

She enters my heart

and knows her way around and says:

"Yes,

everything in here makes sense."

She cups my soul in her wrinkled hands

and kneads out the ache

with oils peppermint scented.

She kisses and caresses my words,

my clumsy,

lum-

bering words

and gives them

voice -

shape -

life –

power!

Only with her is this possible:

words I could never say,

but she helps me

put

to paper.

Stillbirths

Some poems come to life

at the most inopportune times!

There was nothing that could be done.

While I am driving in the rain alone

lines of poetry land on my tongue

like birds on a wire.

Temporary.

Conceived, but never born.

There was nothing that could be done.

Just so many of them.

The cup

When I had a toothache as a child,

you improvised,

rubbed Jamaican rum on my gums;

it soothed the pain with a flavorful numbness

making me smell like my uncle's breath

at parties.

Years later

a jellyfish would sting me at Lido Beach

and you would pour a beer on my leg

to disinfect it.

In our house,

a tall glass of ice cold soda

was always the cure

for mental or physical exasperation.

I was taught from a young age

that the first thing that touches a person's lips

in the morning

is a strong cup of coffee:

the breakfast of champions.

And in my 20's,

when my engagement to be married

was announced

and then broken,

we drank wine together

from what seemed like a bottomless barrel.

Ginger ale,

OJ,

Pinot Grigio.

having you as my father,

my cup runneth over.

Brother

After all the tickle fights and tennis matches and

underwater summersaults:

resentment.

Set a good example,

you're the first born.

he looks up to you:

copies everything you do.

Made a momma's boy to satiate our mother:

coddled and catered to

until she the day she died.

And on the day she died—

that boy,

already a man—

wandered the NICU of the world

with his broken heart inside his chest

never getting to see a nurse,

because he looked so strong.

Time passes. Time heals.

Wife, life, daughter, son, daughter.

And suddenly, a friendship grew.

Heroes are expected to save others,

but not all of

them have to save themselves first.

After our family changed forever,

leaving only three

roommates:

pride.

You set a good example.

You're the second born.

I look up to you:

while I don't copy everything you do like making

pasta sandwiches and putting ketchup on my eggs,

I tell everyone I know about you.

Like mommy used to.

And daddy.

Keep

your eye on the ball.

your knees bent.

your hip to the net.

Keep money in the bank.

gas in your car.

your enemies close.

your childlike spirit.

your heart open.

your wits about you.

what you promise.

your eye on the ball.

Keep trying to talk to her.

praying each night.

telling her you love her.

chasing your dreams.

living and loving.

Keep guiding my actions.

watching my moves.

your eye on me, Dad.

your eye on the ball.

Weekend warrior

This weekend I'm going to save the world.

And paint the living room.

And lose 20 lbs.

I'm going to wake up at dawn
and boil chicken stock
and chop carrots
and celery
and onions
until my fingers are tinged orange
and my eyes are damp and weepy.

This weekend I'm going to color-code my clothes
in my closet so I know what the hell I have.

This weekend.

This weekend I'm going to finally call my friend
from high school
and tell her that I think about her all the time.

I'm going to vacuum my car
and cook dinner for the neighbors
and read all the books in my house.

This weekend.

This weekend I'm going sit down

and finally write
a letter to my mother in heaven and say
the things I never got to say.

And I'm going to find time,

finally this weekend

to do what the therapist said I should do:

Forgive myself.

That—

she said,

should come before all the rest.

I really should wash the windows.
And clean the AC filters.
And oh, there's so much laundry.

Creed

*(title, concept, and structure
"borrowed" from Meg Kearney's "Creed")*

I believe in the Golden Rule. I believe that

there's a design to the universe and that

forgiving someone who hurt you

is harder than you think because

being the person you want to be

and being the person you are

are two different stars in the sky.

I believe in divine evenings spent sifting through

old family photos,

eating slow-churned vanilla bean ice cream,

and that life is not fair,

and that no one ever said it would be

because some bad shit happens to good people.

I believe in the therapeutic effect of re-watching

movies you know by heart,

and that I will watch

Titanic,

The Godfather,

Jaws,

Grease,

and Goodfellas

every time I stumble upon them on TV.

I believe that every time I see Rocky

I will feel the urge to do push-ups

in my living room.

I believe that all people are equal and important,

and that

Every

Living

Thing

Has

A

Soul.

I believe in the soothing, mood-altering

power of a maple syrup-scented

Yankee candle.

I believe in acting as young as you feel

and that Christmas is best spent in New York.

I believe in the sayings:

"what a difference a day makes"

and

"if you slept late, you needed it"

and

"people are funny about money."

I believe in the power of a song to alter the

trajectory of a life.

I believe in loud laughter,

late nights, and

long lasting embraces.

I believe in charity

and in cheesy acts of kindness.

I believe that taking care of at least one animal in

your life makes God truly happy.

I believe that leaving your home is the only way

to find yourself.

I believe in tough love,

but not in love at first sight.

I believe telling girls they can be anything they

want to be is back-asswards.

I believe that giving a child a lollipop because he

survived a doctor's visit is back-asswards.

I believe that having a child you do not want to

make a priority is back-asswards.

I believe that millions out there desperately want

to love your baby,

because they can't have their own.

I believe in leaving your comfort zone in the dust

and that

the ones who want it the most deserve it.

I believe that fear is crippling.

I believe in the awe-inspiring, never exhausted

promise of America,

and that they hate us cause they ain't us.

I believe in talking on the phone for hours on

end, and in writing notes and passing them, and

in finding fitness every day, and in giant handfuls

of popcorn at the movies, and in swimming too

far out into the ocean. I believe "You've made

your bed, now lie in it."

I believe once a cheater –

always a cheater. I believe that narcissists truly

hate themselves. I believe in saying I'm sorry

and in throwing surprise parties and in being

generous just because. I believe in burning the

midnight oil to get it perfect, and in caring

enough to go the extra mile,

and in trying to answer

the call we hear in our hearts.

I believe we all die unsatisfied

with ourselves.

And I believe

in the healing power

of writing

these words.

Reboot

Reboot the system; refresh the page.

Bluescreen of death; I'm totally frozen.

Find time for you; says the sage.

Regretting everything I've ever chosen.

A flurry of files, folders brings relief—

Keeping busy with what others need.

Welcome distractions from feeling my grief.

From what in life is never guaranteed.

I've changed my password many times over

I don't even have access to myself.

Sometimes I don't feel open, but covered.

I'd prefer to be left upon that shelf.

Warning: your password can't stay the same.

Time to try a new username.

Some

Some poetry feels too good.

Like late afternoon sun,

springtime springing

and sweet validation.

You feel almost guilty experiencing it.

A devilish finger slides itself through decadent

chocolate frosting on a cupcake

making its way quickly onto your tongue

before

anyone

sees.

Some poems are like that.

Some poetry feels too right.

Like you're not just reading words on a page,

but you're meeting a friend

whom you should have been friends with

this whole time.

But it's a poem, not a new-old friend,

so you just read it

and eat it,

and let it nourish you.

Some poetry stops you in your tracks.

It humbles, hurts, and haunts.

You shout, stare, perhaps slap the desk

with a flat palm.

And some poetry just baffles you:

Like the DOW JONES INDUSTRIAL AVERAGE

or how some people go jogging

at 4:30 in the morning

or the Spanish soap operas when they talk too

fast and you try and try—

but you can't keep up.

Homework

I keep telling myself:

Give me gravel and dirt;

save my respite and glory for later.

Now is reserved for blood, sweat, and tears.

Taking the tougher road; I have for years.

Early mornings, long days, thankless favors.

Success "counted sweetest" is I what I will savor.

So, pile it on—I don't need a break.

My strength is real; nothing here is fake.

Tedious travels, endless chores, busy nights.

Nothing's for free; I welcome the fight.

I didn't get a million dollar head start.

I've worked for every nickel and dime I've got.

One day,

I'll take home all the glory.

The best part should come at the end of a story.

Marks

What will I do with my time on earth?

What will I make my little life worth?

What have I done since my day of birth?

Have I yet found that talisman

for which we all search?

We all get 24 hours a day

to find our voices;

what we want to say.

To shape our tomorrows; to find our way.

What did I accomplish today?

Why is it some people paint the sky?

Write the novels that make us cry?

Leave indelible marks before they die?

Are you satisfied?

A Mere pebble

Equipped with only one life,

a mere pebble given to me to toss where I wish,

or to keep in my pocket,

selfish,

I seek out a summit

and propel it out

and upward,

giving it wings.

How will I be remembered?

What footprint will I leave?

How far will my impact reach?

Equipped with only one life,

I choose to teach.

Fantasy

I live another life in my imagination:

an existence of visceral emotion

and endless pleasures.

In my mind's eye your face appears

and it rescues me

from the now,

from the real,

from the today,

from the never to be.

I escape into a dream and

float

to a fragile,

ephemeral place

built on veils of reverie and rainbows:

a stage on which there is only one actor

and one director.

The scene opens; the fleeting story unfolds.

And the light in your eyes dances,

and the joy on your face grows

slowly

into a guileless smile

where innocence abounds,

and you let out a laugh—so pure—

 that it gives me the strength to live another day

of the real charade—

once this curtain closes.

Treading Shallow Waters

Puritan

There's something about a man

who vacuums on Saturdays.

A woman who stays in on the weekends to write.

A child who practices piano for hours,

reads books not required.

There's something about a man

who paints in his apartment

hoping one day

some of these simple strokes will ease

the ache

in his

heart

or someone else's.

Why is it that some of us strive to hear

symphonies in the silence,

And have epiphanies in the dark?

Student-athlete

He carries himself with a subtle confidence—

humble,

but proud

that in days to come,

crowds will cry his name.

His head is clear

and in the moment;

his back tired, sore, but strong.

There's sincerity in his smile.

His legs possess an ache today that's honest.

The hours fly by and he shows all his work in

math class;

takes a Spanish test.

Camino del exito.

Like the soundtrack to his day,

he hears the replay

of his coach's voice in his head.

He exists as one among brothers.

With the rising sun,

all his hurts will heal

and serve his spirit well—

when his insatiable eyes

hunt again for glory on the ice:

Tomorrow, he will tear victory

from his opponents' hands

leaving them,

no—

everyone—

incredulous.

Once

Once...

I saw this neighborhood kid's mom come out of her house in just her bathing suit. She was wearing a royal blue one piece and flip-flops, and her hair was all messy in a bun, and her shoes flip-flopped on the driveway as she dragged the garbage pail back up from the curb with a cigarette in one hand and the Rubbermaid pail in the other.

When she reached her house again, I
heard her mumbling.

And once,
I saw that same neighborhood kid's dad walking home from the train station carrying his brief case and wearing sneakers instead of shoes.

 I asked him:

Is your car broken? and he said no.

And I said why are you walking?

And he said exercise.

And I said oh.

And once,

I saw my teacher in her jacket after school, ready

to leave, her suit over her arm. She had put on

yoga pants and a sweatshirt, and her husband

had come to pick her up.   I saw my teacher's

husband, who wore glasses and had dark, curly

hair.

He looked just like Uncle Len.

Once I read a book where the author included

her rough draft and notes in the paperback copy.

And once I asked to go to the bathroom at the

store and the cashier took me to the break room.

The paper towels needed to be changed and

there was black sharpie on the wall that said

Andrea was here.

And once

I saw my principal cry—

and not a little cry, but the kind that

makes your neck red and blotchy,

hurts your insides,

and stifles speech.

And I got to thinking:

Who saw me

un-showered,

run to the supermarket Christmas Eve morning

that time I needed

parsley and

brown sugar

and mostly—

time alone?

Youth

Bubbly, quick-witted, confident spitfire.

Endless possibilities and adventures await you—

friendships,

lovers,

triumphs,

glory days,

road trips,

one night stands,

hangovers,

lost weekends,

experimentation,

self-discovery,

genuine happiness,

peace.

New Jersey

(inspired by and modeled after
"Harlem"
by Langston Hughes)

What happens to a dream we adore?
Does it take flight like a rocket and soar?
Or reign majestic like a lion and roar?

What happens to a dream
we passionately pursue?
Our faith, does it renew?
Does it come true?

Maybe it keeps our fire alive,
our motivation to strive;
our eyes on a prize.

Or maybe it gives us direction and purpose.
Making sacrifice worth it,
as we toil to unearth it.

What happens to a dream in which we believe?
Is it achieved?

Four letter words

Want: huge come back.

Wait: time will heal.

This hard time will pass.

Come back home.

Rest.

Don't shed that tear.

Grab hold next year.

Have zero fear.

With hope, cope.

Pass this test.

Someday you'll find it

We all search—

every living thing.

The finch—

for the fork of a tree.

For pollen, the bee.

The Beagle,

you,

and me.

We all search.

We live looking and searching –

for this

for that,

for keys.

For love,

for inspiration,

for success,

for pride,

for purpose,

for the reason why.

For God.

And I ask you: then what?

Cobalt world

My foot lands

on gray, weathered, cobblestone streets.

As I leave this world,

I tread on ancient lands now

as if I am light as air,

carried,

almost whisked

by the healing hands of unencumbered time.

The night air is frosty cold;

holds the flavor of snow.

I clutch my coat to my chest,

my brown leather gloves

still lying on the arm of a chair at home

instead of sheathing my chapped hands now.

I hear a baby crying

from inside a stranger's home.

The child's parents try soothing him

in a language

I both do

and don't understand.

I let the foreign tongue of the mother speak to

me until I am her baby.

I breathe it all in

and

fill

my

lungs

with good fortune and gratitude and love.

On this bitter night in Europe I feel fortunate.

I rejoice and whisper, like monks and poets do.

At my feet, a piece of

cobalt glass sits forgotten about

between two stones.

I want to show the world my discovery,

but I keep it to myself.

It seems put just there for me

along with

the solitude,

the peacefulness,

the serenity,

the tranquility.

Save for a few black cats rummaging for gold,

I am alone

in this hallucinogenic world

with my treasure.

Feral

The feline's stare is keenly focused.

Her senses attentive.

Water pools in her mouth.

Her eyes, alert—

 as piercing as a lighthouse beam.

She has spotted her prey

and all else in the universe dissipates

around her now,

melting

like abandoned butter

on a butcher-block countertop.

The earth goes silent: slows to a still.

It would be a tragedy

(for you)

to disturb her now.

Countless victims have been caught

in the deception

fashioned by

her powdery soft fur,

her seductive purr,

her welcoming pose,

her heart-shaped nose.

Take heed and let her be.

She knows no loyalty.

Insulting perhaps, but true:

She has, for this moment,

forgotten the name you call her.

She hears nothing but her ancestors' teachings;

As instinct whispers in her ear.

An ode to mothers

Her weary feet hit the floor early,

eyes still salty from sleep,

yet watchful not to wake the others.

Motherhood is not a hobby of hers,

or a chore,

or a lifestyle—

it's her religion.

She is the CEO of the household;

The hero of the home.

She's the only one who always knows where things are.

Scotch tape,

the ketchup,

that white shirt that looks so good with these jeans.

When you ask her for a scissor she replies,

"you want the new one or the old one with the red handle?"

Christmas presents are burrowed away in corners of her bedroom

waiting to be wrapped.

  It is only September.

From her altar, the kitchen counter, she

performs healing rituals with as little as

chicken and rice.

Her son is convinced

she's the only one in the world

who knows how to cut his sandwiches.

From the University of Life

she has received

Honorary Degrees in

Adolescent Psychology,

Home Economics,

Cooking,

Organization,

and Common Sense.

You hope to be like her someday,

and you will be.

You are one of her cubs

trained well for the wild.

Lemonade

Serenity stretches like a protective sheath

over everything.

A stolen Sunday lets families

look at one another in the eye.

Sailboats, like dreams,

float

unthreatened of never coming true,

for they are true.

The radio reported

still waters and clouds;

not enough sunshine for some

who choose to wait

for the perfect day to take to the harbor.

But I say

temperature is only part

of what makes lemonade so sweet.

All I hear—

and ever want to hear

are birds

and laughter

and children.

Today,

like lemonade,

doesn't have to be perfect

to be perfect.

Things are

I'm a little girl

trying to stop rain drops

with her bare hands.

The path stars take has been forever planned.

Man cannot stand

in feeble opposition to the clouds

as they seemingly sift

and shift

indifferently through the air.

Things are as they are—

And what of it?

We cannot build a wall against the wind

and blow it back from where it came

and never have it find us again.

Things are as they are.

Our breath is better spent on ourselves;

for we are not moon-catchers.

Even giants must acquiesce to the rain

and lift their palms

in humble welcome.

The power of zero

Love could never mean zero.

Growing up on the courts at the school yard,

it's something I could never understand.

Love is not nothingness;

an empty void;

it's the pulsating magnetic energy that

mesmerizes and inspires.

Love is not a car in neutral,

a device switched to OFF,

it's the black and white photographs at the

foundation of our families;

the fabric that binds our very lives

and souls together;

the stories passed down

from generation

to generation

about survivors

and heroes

and best-friends

and newlyweds.

Love could never mean zero.

It heals and helps.

It soothes and satisfies.

Love brings home dinner, takes out the trash,

and sets up coffee for tomorrow

so you don't have to.

Love sits and stays.

Love calls you back;

says just the right things

at just the right time

and never intentionally hurts you.

Love could never mean zero

because

zero is one less

than

the

loneliest

number.

A letter-less mailbox;

something not yet started.

Love has power!

What power does a zero have?

I write a zero next to my age

and I am 460 years old.

I write a zero next to my salary,

and I am the richest graduate

of the class of '89.

I draw a zero and what do I see?

The hug missing its kiss— XO.

The initial outline of a face.

Perhaps a ring circling round and round:

absolute infinity.

So, what if love does mean zero.

Zero conditions,

zero excuses,

zero cruelty,

zero apologies,

zero pain,

zero end.

No presence of negative in either direction;

No absence of positive.

The very beginning.

Always a new beginning.

Lift

She asked her dejection

only one question:

Do I have any lift left

or am I beat?

And with some reflection,

she made the connection:

This shift must be made from my seat.

Not ready to die—

she took to the sky—

put the clouds under her feet.

Treading Shallow Waters

MELLENE HEDERIAN

Made in the USA
Columbia, SC
13 June 2021